K-POP

THE ULTIMATE
FAN BOOK

YOUR ESSENTIAL GUIDE TO ALL
THE HOTTEST K-POP BANDS

MALCOLM CROFT

STERLING CHILDREN'S BOOKS
New York

CONTENTS

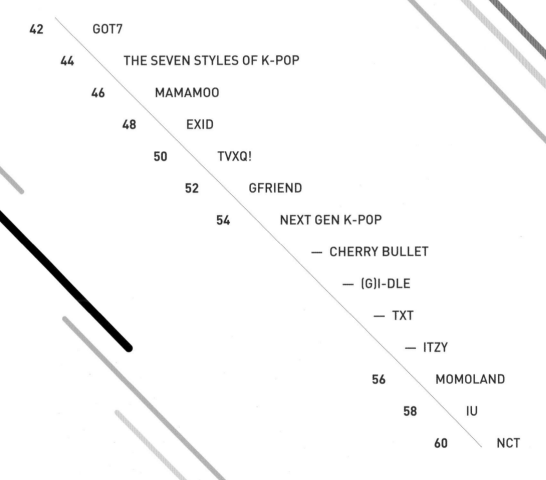

HELLO HALLYU!

As we slide into the second decade of the 21st century, there is just one fact that we all know to be true: K-Pop rules the world. It's taken its sweet time to get here—its origins date back more than two decades, after all—but now that it has, fans from (almost) every country on Earth are devouring every *maknae* and *hyung* that comes along.

In the more than 20 years since it first came to mainstream attention on Korean TV, pop music from South Korea was held at the border of its host nation, remaining a relatively local phenomenon, occasionally breaking free and allowing the world to see what talents lay hidden in that often overlooked part of the atlas.

Today, Korean pop music is a global obsession, pioneering a path forward for all Asian music to be heard without prejudice on the world's airwaves, unlike ever before in music history. Tomorrow, aspiring popstars, rock stars, and superstars—and the future victors of the pop charts—will no longer be singing predominantly in English, the world's musical language, but in Korean, and other Asian languages. Because right now, K-Pop is devoured wherever it is desired, spreading around the globe as quickly as you can snap your fingers.

And, phew, there are hundreds—if not thousands!—of incredible K-Pop, rock, and hip-hop groups to tickle your ears with, both classic and old school as well as fresh out of the oven and baking hot today.

With its breathtaking dance acrobatics and razor-sharp choreography, infectious melodies, anthemic hooks, and high concept MVs—all driven by genuine in-group chemistry—K-Pop has everything a fan could want. It's perfection, just as the idols strive for.

This ultimate fan book takes you as close to the groups as you want to be and throws a bright spotlight on the idols and icons that have propelled K-Pop from the periphery of the

world's lens into sharp 4K focus. From Astro to Monsta X, and (not quite) everyone in between, the groups that embody K-Pop come in all shapes and sizes, from solo artists and duos, to groups with more than twenty rotating members, each one as distinct, defined, and dazzling as the next. Your new favorite K-Pop group lives inside this book. The only thing you have to decide is where to start. Happy K-Popping!

ABOVE K-Pop pioneers Big Bang paved the way for the genre's dominance.

K-POP GLOSSARY

A group member's cute behavior is called **Aegyo**. Jungkook, obviously, has this mastered.

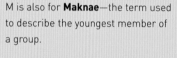

K-Pop is famous for MVs, or **Music Videos**. Psy's "Gangnam Style" is the best, but B.A.P's "One Shot" is the most expensive. Check it out!

B is for **Bias**, or your favorite member of your favorite K-Pop group.

M is also for **Maknae**—the term used to describe the youngest member of a group.

K-Pop groups are famous for making yearly **Comebacks**, usually with the release of multiple EPs or trilogies.

Nugus are idol groups that are relatively unpopular or unknown. But don't call anyone Nugu—it's rude!

Entertainment companies, such as JYP, YG, SM, and Big Hit, are the record labels and management agencies that put K-Pop groups together, hire producers and songwriters, and operate every part of a K-Pop group's success.

All new (under two years) K-Pop groups are known as **Rookies**. If your group finds success early, such as NCT and Blackpink, you become **Monster Rookies**!

Fandoms! Every group has its fans who devour everything they do, and each have their own awesome name. BTS have their Army, Blackpink have their Blinks. What fandom do you belong to?

Sasaengs are obsessed fans who will do anything to get close to their favorite groups.

K-Pop is one of the main ingredients of **Hallyu**, or Korean Wave. Hallyu has been used since 1999 to describe all of Korea's cultural exports, including television and movies.

Many new groups, such as NCT, for example, can be divided into **Sub-units**, in which individual members within a group form a separate smaller unit.

Hyung is a Korean word that means "older brother," and used by a younger, member to describe elder members of a group.

Trainees are wannabe idols who sign with an entertainment company and train, usually for several years, in the hope they become fully fledged idols.

An **Idol** is what you become when you successfully audition and become a member of a group.

 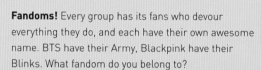

THE
BIG BANG!

Since its earliest incarnations, K-Pop has appeared to its super fans in sets of waves. The first generation began (way back) in the 1990s when American hip-hop was first broadcast on Korean TV, inspiring millions of Koreans to follow their dreams of becoming an idol. Today, K-Pop is big business, and the next generation of groups are breaking through the noise in the hope of becoming worldwide superstars. It all started here...

1995

SM Entertainment is founded by Lee Soo-man. Over the years, the company found success with Kangta, S.E.S., BoA, TVXQ!, TraxX, CSJH The Grace, Super Junior (below), Girls' Generation, J-Min, SHINee, f(x), Zhou Mi, EXO, Red Velvet, NCT, and more!

1997

JYP Entertainment is founded by former pop songwriter Park Jin-young. The agency creates popular groups such as Got7, Rain, Wonder Girls (below), 2PM, and 2AM.

1996

H.O.T. (Highfive of Teenagers), K-Pop's first idol group, are formed. In five years, they sell more than six million records in South Korea.

1997

S.E.S., K-Pop's first all-girl group, are signed by SM Entertainment. They are the leading group in K-Pop's "Big 3" girl groups, with Fin.K.L and Baby V.O.X.

2000

Hallyu—the first wave of South Korean music and culture—becomes globally recognized.

2001

MTV Korea is launched, playing 24 hours of South Korean pop music.

2008

Rain appear on the *Colbert Report* in the United States—and are the first group to crack the notoriously difficult American market.

2009

Girls' Generation release "Gee"—the first big global K-Pop classic. It would become the first K-Pop song to reach 100 million views on YouTube in 2013.

2009

BoA, the "Queen of K-Pop," became the first K-Pop artist to enter the Billboard Top 200.

2011

Billboard establishes the Korea Top Hot 100 chart. Sistar's "So Cool" was the first song to be top of the pops.

2012

Psy's (below) "Gangnam Style" became a global viral phenomenon, kick-starting the world's obsession with K-Pop.

2012

Girls' Generation perform "The Boys" on the popular *Late Night with David Letterman* in the US, the first girl group to perform on a highly influential American TV show.

2012

The first ever K-Pop convention, KCON, is launched in California.

2013

Psy wins a Billboard Music Award for "Gangnam Style"—the most watched video of the year—with more than one billion views!

2014

BTS (below) play their first US concert at Los Angeles' nightclub, the Troubadour... and begin the ascent to global superstardom.

2015

EXO release Exodus and become the biggest K-Pop export to the US... so far!

2015

2NE1's CL goes solo and releases the worldwide hit single "Hello Bitches."

2016

Epik High become the first K-Pop act to perform at the super-cool and influential Coachella Music Festival in California.

2016

Blackpink become the fastest-selling K-Pop group with "Boombayah" and "Whistle."

2016

BTS rule the world and become the first K-Pop group to top the Billboard Social 50 chart. They win again in 2018.

2017

BTS win Top Social Artist at the Billboard Music Awards, displacing Justin Bieber for the first time in six years.

2017

BTS's *Love Yourself: Her* debuts in the Top 10 album charts all over the world.

2018

BTS perform on the *Tonight Show starring Jimmy Fallon* in the US.

2019

Blackpink's single "Kill This Love" smashes YouTube records, becoming the fastest music video to surpass 100 million YouTube views, in less than three days. It's also the first song by a girl group to reach No.1 on iTunes in the US since Destiny's Child in 2004.

THE FIRST WAVE:
CLASSIC K-POP

From its earliest hip-hop and rock influences, to today's laser-precision neon pop, K-Pop is constantly evolving within its own clearly defined parameters. To many, it was Psy who, in 2012, kick-started the K-Pop trend. But it was, in fact, the idol acts who broke out in the 1990s that began the phenomenon.

If you're not sure where to begin your K-Pop journey, or are looking for some old-school classics, look no further: these are some of the groups that first defined K-Pop... and helped put everyone's favorite new musical genre firmly on the global map.

RAIN

Rain (real name: Jung Ji-Hoon) was the first K-Pop artist to find fame outside Korea, a huge achievement for the fledgling musical and social movement at the time. 1998 was the year when he debuted with his boy group, Fanclub. They split up two years later, but Rain was clearly not going to stop or fall, so he released his solo album, N001, in 2002. He would go on to have rain-based hits with 2004's It's Raining and 2008's Rainism. When it rains, it pours, after all.

Today, Rain remains one of the most famous South Korean singer-songwriters, producers, and actors, starring in several Hollywood and Asian movies. In 2007, Rain was even named Time magazine's most influential person in the world, beating Beyoncé! He said at the time: "I would really like to see an Asian make it in the United States... and I would like that Asian to be me!" His dream came true.

TOP 10 RAIN MVs
1. FREE WAY
2. HOW TO AVOID THE SUN
3. I DO
4. HANDSHAKE
5. BAD GUY
6. 30 SEXY
7. THE BEST PRESENT
8. LOVE STORY
9. IT'S RAINING
10. RAINISM

TOP 10 SEO TAIJI MVs

1. SAD PAIN
2. GOODBYE
3. ETERNITY
4. ANYHOW SONG
5. MUST TRIUMPH
6. YOU, IN THE FANTASY
7. TO YOU
8. COME BACK HOME
9. DREAMING OF BAL-HAE
10. I KNOW

SEO TAIJI AND BOYS

In 2017, Seo Taiji stood on stage in Seoul with BTS—the biggest boy band in the world—and declared, "This is your generation now." The baton had finally been passed.

It is widely acknowledged that K-Pop began on April 11, 1992, when Seo Taiji and Boys, a hip-hop trio (with Yang Hyunsuk and Lee Juno), performed their debut rap-rock single "I Know" on a talent show on South Korean TV. They were an overnight sensation.

Inspired by American hip-hop, heavy metal, and rock, Seo Taiji and Boys were completely original, at once challenging and changing society, fusing together high-energy dancing with heavy hip-hop and rock tunes. During their tenure, Seo Taiji and Boys eventually changed censorship laws, allowing second and third generation K-Pop acts to follow in their massive footsteps. The floodgates were now open! Seo Taiji became a cultural icon of Korea, earning the prestigious title of "President of Culture." Fellow member, Yang Hyunsuk, formed YG Entertainment, producers of Blackpink and Big Bang, and one of the largest talent agencies in Korea.

GIRLS' GENERATION

With bubblegum pop songs as colorful as their neon stage costumes, it came as little surprise that Girls Generation's debut in 2007 was a wish come true for their fans, known as "SONE" (pronounced "so-won," which means "wish" in Korean). In less than five years, this stunning octet with big ambitions took the K-Pop world by storm, becoming the first group to perform a song ("The Boys") on a US late night talk show (*The Late Show with David Letterman*)—a now-compulsory appearance for any hot K-Pop act wanting to break the internet. Members Taeyeon, Sunny, Tiffany, Hyoyeon, Yuri, Sooyoung, Yoona, and Seohyun, first found fame with their glorious single "Gee," now regarded as a K-Pop classic, but have had a string of hits deserving of their incredible vocal talents ever since. At home, the girls are regarded as "The Nation's Girl Group." Abroad, in 2017, the girls were honored by *Billboard*, the U.S.'s most esteemed music magazine, as the best K-Pop Girl Group of the Past Decade. We couldn't agree more!

TOP 10 GIRLS GENERATION MVs

1. TELL ME YOUR WISH (GENIE)
2. I GOT A BOY
3. GEE
4. MR MR
5. CATCH ME IF YOU CAN
6. RUN DEVIL RUN
7. PAPARAZZI
8. INTO THE NEW WORLD
9. GIRL'S GENERATION
10. OH!

H.O.T.

In 1996, following hot on the heels of Seo Taiji and Boys' success, came five-piece H.O.T., K-Pop's first idol group, created by SM Entertainment. As an acronym for Highfive of Teenagers, it is H.O.T. who established the formula for K-Pop's current success, which many of today's generation still strictly adhere to. The group were formed in training sessions conducted by SM, and the final selected idols were Moon Hee-joon, Jang Woo-hyuk, Tony An, Kangta, and Lee Jae-won. This winning combination would go onto sell more than six million records in Asia, becoming the first superstars of Hallyu—the Korean Wave.

The group went cold in 2001, but enjoyed a successful comeback in 2018. "We have expanded the spectrum of the K-Pop market," said Tony An in 2018. "We didn't mean to set the trend. We had no choice but to grow the market by ourselves and did what we did best. The K-Pop market was born along the way." H.O.T.—we salute you!

TOP 10 H.O.T. MVs
1. WARRIOR'S DESCENDANT
2. CANDY
3. WOLF AND SHEEP
4. FULL OF HAPPINESS
5. WE ARE THE FUTURE
6. LINE UP
7. HOPE
8. I YAH!
9. IT'S BEEN RAINING SINCE YOU LEFT ME
10. WE CAN DO IT

TOP 10 SUPER JUNIOR MVs
1. DEVIL
2. IN MY DREAM
3. DON'T DON'T
4. NO OTHER
5. SEXY, FREE AND SINGLE
6. BITTERSWEET
7. IT'S YOU
8. SORRY SORRY
9. EVANESCE
10. MR. SIMPLE

SUPER JUNIOR

Debuting in 2005, Super Junior are still going... well, super! They may be old (okay, 30!), but they remain relevant despite the youth-dominated purchasing power of K-Pop. The group originally comprised 13 members—Leeteuk, Heechul, Hangeng, Yesung, Kangin, Shindong, Sungmin, Eunhyuk, Siwon, Donghae, Ryeowook, Kibum, and Kyuhyun, but lost some members along the way. The group became famous for their highly acrobatic and high energy choreography, as well as anthemic, addictive songs, "Sorry Sorry," being the big one, charting in the United States in 2009 and going viral online, which was an achievement considering YouTube was still in its infancy back then. They held the honor of being the bestselling K-Pop group four years in a row, though BTS have now broken that record by a long way!

"When we first debuted, this word 'K-Pop' it wasn't such a big phenomenon as it is now," said band leader Leeteuk in 2018. "But when we started to get really popular with 'Sorry Sorry,' K-Pop as a whole became such a huge sensation. We want to continue to grow as a group, so that when the public thinks 'K-Pop,' Super Junior becomes a household name that is very much relevant to 'K-Pop.'"

SUPER JUNIOR FANS ARE CALLED E.L.F.s—EVER LASTING FRIENDS!

BIG BANG

One of K-Pop's most influential and most popular second-generation groups is the aptly titled Big Bang. First debuted in 2007 on YG Entertainment, Big Bang became one of the first supergroups of K-Pop to play their genre-busting songs to stadiums in the U.S. The four-piece consists of G-Dragon, T.O.P, Taeyang, and Daesung, after fifth member Seungri left the entertainment industry in 2019. Each member is personally involved in contributing to the group's musical output, as well as stage routines and individual sense of style, a rare treat for early K-Pop. They first received worldwide recognition in 2011, winning Best Worldwide Act at the inaugural 2011 MTV Europe Music Awards. But it was with their third album *Made* (2016)—a critical and commercial smash—that they cemented themselves as the "Kings of K-Pop," a fact backed up by selling more than 140 million records, making them one of the biggest-selling boy groups not just in Korea... but the whole world. "It's clear that not only in Asia, but that many people from countries across the globe love Big Bang and K-Pop," said G-Dragon in 2015 from the stage of their record-breaking Korean tour—the biggest tour the country has ever seen... so far!

TOP 10 BIG BANG MVs

1. BANG BANG BANG
2. THE LAST FAREWELL
3. MONSTER
4. FXXK IT
5. LOVE SONG
6. BAD BOY
7. LET'S NOT FALL IN LOVE
8. LIES
9. HARU HARU
10. FANTASTIC BABY

TOP 10 S.E.S. MVs

1. U
2. TWILIGHT ZONE
3. SHY BOY
4. LOVE
5. I LOVE YOU
6. BE NATURAL
7. JUST A FEELING
8. DREAMS COME TRUE
9. I'M YOUR GIRL
10. PARADISE

S.E.S.

Widely regarded as K-Pop's first major successful all-girl group, S.E.S. first debuted on the scene in November 1997, as part of SM Entertainment's roster, and as the first female counterpoint to the highly successful boy idol group H.O.T. S.E.S.'s name is taken from their members first names—Shoo, Eugene, and Sea—with each member identified as singer, rapper, and dancer respectively.

While the group disbanded in 2002, their return in 2016 is considered the greatest first generation group comeback in K-Pop to date, with the song 'Three Words' and album *Remember*, which outsold many current K-Pop groups new releases. "I think a lot of people were happy to hear that we were coming back," said Shoo, of the comeback. "I'm having fun... I dreamed of meeting my fans after we separated, so our comeback is very meaningful!"

WONDER GIRLS

Breaking out in 2007, the Wonder Girls are exactly what their name suggests! As one of the longest surviving K-Pop acts, there is hardly anywhere the Wonder Girls haven't wandered. Created by JYP Entertainment, the quintet of Sunye, Yeeun, Sunmi, Hyuna (later replaced by Yubin), and Sohee, dropped their debut album, *The Wonder Years* in 2007, and their killer debut single "Tell Me," which recalled the "retro" musical genres of the 1960s, 70s, and 80s. "We all auditioned, some of us were trained in an academy," said Sunye of their fierce idol training. "We went to a regular school, and after school we trained in vocal and dance lessons. We learned singing, dancing, acting, and language. Once a month there would be a test, like a talent show." In 2009, Wonder Girls became the first South Korean group to enter the U.S. charts with the song "Nobody." Ironically, the song made them somebodies almost instantly! The song also helped them gain the attention of the Jonas Brothers, the famous American trio and biggest group in the US at the time, who offered the group a supporting slot on their world tour, the first time a K-Pop group had received such recognition abroad. The group went their separate ways in 2017, but there will always be a space in their fans' hearts for K-Pop's one and only "retro queens."

TOP 10 WONDER GIRLS MVs

1. THIS FOOL/STUPID
2. SO HOT
3. TELL ME
4. IRONY
5. LIKE THIS
6. NOBODY
7. 2 DIFFERENT TEARS
8. BE MY BABY
9. WHY SO LONELY
10. I FEEL YOU

OPPOSITE 2NE1 perform onstage during the MTV Video Music Awards Japan 2012 at Makuhari Messe.

LEFT More than a decade since their debut, SHINee continue to reign as certified K-Pop royalty.

SHINEE

Debuting in 2008 with a hot slice of K-Pop gold, the song "Replay" gave the four-piece their first big hit—and, more than a decade later, their feet have yet to touch the ground. "In the song's intro, when you hear the heartbeat sound," said vocalist Taemin, "it made me feel like, 'Oh, this is the beginning.' The beginning of SHINEe. The beginning of my life, too." Beloved as the "Princes of K-Pop," SHINEe's members Onew, Key, Minho, and Taemin have a brotherly bond greater than blood—a bond that was cemented in 2017 following the death of their fifth member, Jonghyun.

First introduced as a "contemporary boy band"—and therefore destined to become trend-setters in music, fashion, and dance—it wasn't long before the band started the "SHINee trend" among Korean students and youths. "When we were starting out as the group SHINee, the title of 'contemporary boy band' was added and we concentrated on being a trend leader," recalled Minho. Now, the group transcends trends to be considered one of the best live vocal groups in K-Pop, and the best dancers, too—check out the complex and highly synchronized dance routines of their songs "Sherlock," "Dream Girl," and "View"—breathtaking!

TOP 10 SHINEE MVs

1. LUCIFER
2. REPLAY
3. RING DING DONG
4. SHERLOCK
5. HELLO
6. DREAM GIRL
7. JULIETTE
8. EVERYBODY
9. SYMPTOMS
10. STAND BY ME

TOP 10 2NE1 MVs

1. I AM THE BEST
2. TAKE ON THE WORLD
3. HATE YOU
4. LONELY
5. GOTTA BE YOU
6. MISSING YOU
7. COME BACK HOME
8. GOODBYE
9. CAN'T NOBODY
10. UGLY

2NE1

Bom, CL, Dara, and Minzy were the fantastic four-piece formed by YG Entertainment in 2009. 2NE1 had arrived! They were, to many, the Spice Girls of K-Pop! But don't tell them that! Before they disbanded in 2016, the group were considered the most successful and popular girl group of all time, selling a massive 66 million records! To their fans, known as Blackjacks (can you work out why?), 2NE1 had it all—they were sexy, strong, and fiercely independent, often refusing to act like other girl groups. In their seven-year tenure at the top of the pops, 2NE1 enjoyed all the spoils of success, winning MTV's "Best New Band in the World" award in 2011, as well as being lucky enough to employ the talents of Will.I.Am (from the Black Eyed Peas) to produce their comeback single "Take on the World" in summer 2013. The track was hella lit, and the band remained on fire until CL went solo in 2016.

"ALTHOUGH EVERYONE HAS THEIR OWN CHARACTER, EVERYONE IS DIFFERENT. BUT ONCE WE COME TOGETHER, WE HAVE A SENSE OF UNITY." BOM, 2NE1

PSY

"To the US and the world, I'm just known as some funny song and some funny music, some funny video guy," so said Psy in 2012, the year that he took K-Pop global, thanks to his breakout song, "Gangnam Style." Named after the most expensive neighborhood in Seoul, its unsurprising that the video to this instant K-Pop classic features a now-famous horse dance! At the end of 2012, the video to "Gangnam Style" had reached one billion views—the first video ever to do so. It was official: Psy was the King of YouTube! Since his debut, Psy has continued to release hit songs, including "Gentleman" and "Hangover," though today his music has been eclipsed by the domination of idol groups such as Blackpink and BTS. "There's a lot of variety of musicians in Korea," Psy said in 2012, predicting the future. "I cannot say they are the best in the world, but I can say that Korean artists are really dynamic artists, so I am going to show that from now on. If I have a chance I want to introduce some of my friends." And, true to his word, that is precisely what he did. Without him, K-Pop might never have kicked off.

TOP 10 PSY MVs

1. GANGNAM STYLE
2. GENTLEMAN
3. HANGOVER
4. I LUV IT
5. DADDY
6. KOREA
7. NEW FACE
8. DANCE JOCKEY
9. THE DAY WILL COME
10. WHAT WOULD HAVE BEEN

BTS

Since this septet broke the internet back in 2013, the global fanbase of BTS has blossomed from big to bigger to, well, just plain bonkers! In 2019, the group are not only leading K-Pop's goal of world domination, they are also one of the biggest pop bands to have existed. *EVER!* Only one question remains: where on earth can they go next?

BEYOND THE STARS

BTS have broken music sales records at home in Korea and abroad, most notably the United States, where no other Asian band has broken as big, or as boldly, before. In 2018, their *Burn the Stage* movie was a box office smash. The same year, they toured the world in sold-out stadiums in support of the acclaimed album *Love Yourself: Tear*. Their *Bangtan Bomb* YouTube channel enjoys millions of weekly views thanks to each member's prolific approach to creating content of all shapes and sizes. They've addressed the UN about youth employment and empowerment; they've started their own charity foundation; they're advocates for social justice and mental health. What else? Oh, yeah, and they're style icons, beloved for their fearless attitude to fashion. They have a legion of worldwide fans, called the Army, who have come to crave all of BTS's creative output. In short, BTS have changed the world. But who are they? Let's go behind the scenes and find out...

From oldest to youngest, the band's seven members are Jin, Suga, J-Hope, Rap Monster (RM), Jimin, V, and Jungkook. Each member adds their own separate, but complementary, flavor to the band's sonic style, allowing BTS to flourish as a one-of-a-kind group never seen before in Western music charts and the beaming beacon of the now-established K-Pop movement currently conquering the world. But, as always, it is the band's brotherly bond

RIGHT At the 2019 Grammy Awards in Los Angeles, BTS stood for just one thing: Black Tie and Suits!

"K-POP INCLUDES VIDEOS, CLOTHES, CHOREOGRAPHY, SOCIAL MEDIA. IT IS THE TOTAL ARTS PACKAGE." RM, BTS

ABOVE BTS attend the SBS Super Concert in Taipei, July 2018.

BELOW BTS storm the American Music Awards for the first time in Los Angeles, November 2017.

OVERLEAF The BTS boys display the unique styles that set them apart.

that makes them something truly beyond belief. There may be seven of them, but they think as one.

"We are really unique," Jungkook revealed to *Miss Vogue* in 2019. "We all have our style, so I think we all stand out, but we do make sure that one person doesn't stand out. We each have our own roles and positions in the band and then we work together to make sure we all try hard for the Army."

Famously, to ensure the seven individual members all have a fair say on the many creative and business decisions as they move toward world domination, they play Rock-Paper-Scissor to ensure they all agree unanimously! "BTS is a democracy," says RM, the band's natural leader and co-founder, a fact that has yet to steer the band in the wrong direction.

BOYS THAT SHINE
In April 2019, BTS burned the stage once more with the release of *Map of the Soul: Persona*, the group's fourth Korean album, and a second world tour, commencing with a performance on the US's most famous TV program, *Saturday Night Live*. They were the first K-Pop act ever to play such a prestigious show.

BLACKPINK

Following hot on the heels of BTS's path toward total world domination is Blackpink, the all-girl quartet that debuted in 2016 with the instant K-Pop classics "Boombayah" and "Whistle" from their *Square One EP*. Fusing uptempo electro-pop with booming hip-hop beats, Blackpink found mega success in 2018 with their collaboration with Dua Lipa, the year's breakout star, on "Kiss and Make Up." Their follow-up, "Ddu-du Ddu-du," unsurprisingly, became the most-viewed music video by a K-Pop group on YouTube, with 750 million views and counting. Take that, BTS!

FOUR GIRLS FOREVER

Jennie, Rosé, Lisa, and Jisoo began making music together in 2016, after being brought together as trainee idols by YG Entertainment. The Seoul-based talent agency and record label responsible for many other K-Pop acts, including K-Pop legend Psy—the first K-Pop act to break out globally—and 2NE1, another all-girl group.

With acclaimed hitmaker and K-Pop producer Teddy Park by their side in the studio, Blackpink have been allowed to bang out some absolute belters, culminating in all their debut singles being brought together for the first time for the Japanese studio album *In Your Area*, released in 2018. Their second album *Kill This Love* followed up in 2019. As Jennie says: "We want to make a full album to really express ourselves. To have a story in an album could be fun, something we haven't tried yet. We've been working on it very hard!"

While creating the final Korean and Japanese versions of the group's songs, Park and the band ensure they include many English phrases and verses so as to make the tracks accessible both for their Asian fans, and the rest of the world. "Teddy knows there are a lot of fanbases around the world that are just waiting on our songs, so I've seen him try to target those people," Rosé revealed in 2018. "Lisa spits out English raps, and he always comes up with cool phrases, because we're trying to take care of everyone listening to our music. I really respect that about our producer. He's very considerate of our fans around the world."

> "OUR GROUP NAME HAS A DUAL MEANING. BLACK MEANING STRONG AND BEING CONFIDENT, AND PINK REPRESENTING THE FEMININE SIDE OF OUR GROUP." JENNIE, BLACKPINK

ABOVE Blackpink caused chaos when they showed up at the 2016 Asia Artist Awards in Seoul, November 2016.

INDEPENDENT WOMEN

While Blackpink are tipped to top the Asian, Billboard, and European charts in 2019, it is the individual release of the four girls' solo records that will help catapult Blackpink the brand into the stardom stratosphere—the first K-Pop band to release both solo and group efforts at the same time.

Of course, this came as no surprise to the band's loyal and loving fans—known as Blinks or Blinkers—who have always known that Blackpink is a group of independent women, performers who worked on their solo careers on top of group work while in idol training. "We all had to know how to perform on our own, that's always been there," says Jennie. "And when we started recording with Teddy, he said, 'You can't always depend on each other –you have to know how to fill up a song by yourself.'"

Being both solo and group recording artists will help the four girls discover themselves and help the band stay fresh and unique in the now ever-expanding K-Pop universe. Jennie Kim was the first to release a solo single, called "Solo" (strangely enough!) In November 2018. The accompanying music video taught Jennie a lot about being an artist, especially about the importance of style. "I really enjoyed putting all the outfits and the whole look together," she says. "That's what I learned a lot about, putting outfits together for the dancers and myself. How will it go with this song? What could I do different? It's not just about the song, it's really everything else within." But, don't worry Blinkers, no matter how big the girls get on their own, they'll always come back together!

THE FUTURE IS BRIGHT

Diving head-first into 2019, to capitalize on their stellar year, in January, Blackpink announced that they will be the first female K-Pop group to perform at Coachella Festival, in California on April 12 and 19, the same month they took their much-anticipated *In Your Area World* Tour across North America, Europe, and Australia. The sky really is the limit for these four stars!

TOP The girls broke all the rules on *The Late Show with Stephen Colbert*, February 2019. They were the first ever K-Pop group to appear on such a revered US TV show.

ABOVE Blackpink—in sync!

BLACKPINK ESSENTIAL PLAYLIST

1. WHISTLE
2. KISS AND MAKE UP
3. BOOMBAYAH
4. DDU-DU DDU-DU
5. STAY
6. AS IF IT'S YOUR LAST
7. FOREVER YOUNG
8. REALLY
9. PLAYING WITH FIRE
10. SEE YOU LATER

THE MASTERS OF
K-POP

K-Pop idols in South Korea are created by entertainment and talent agencies, one-stop shops that oversee the development of aspiring singers and dancers into trainees and, hopefully one day, into proper idols and idol groups, capable of world domination. There are four major agencies responsible for creating idols—YG, SM, Big Hit, and JYP.

YG ENTERTAINMENT

Founded in 1996 by Yang Hyun-suk (below), YG Entertainment does it all: record label, talent agency, music production company, event management and concert production company, and even music publishing house. Many idols, and idol groups, have been created here, including Epik High, 1TYM, 2NE1, Psy, Big Bang, CL, Winner, iKon, and Blackpink.

BIG HIT ENTERTAINMENT

Bang Si-hyuk (right), the man responsible for BTS, founded Big Hit in 2005. Currently, Big Hit only manages two artists—BTS and TXT. One is the biggest band in the world, and the other is about to be, so no doubt they're still very busy.

"I'M THE KING OF SURFING THE INTERNET. IT'S MY JOB TO KNOW WHAT PEOPLE WHO DON'T LIKE BTS HAVE TO SAY, WHAT PEOPLE WANT FROM BTS, WHAT I CAN DO FOR THEM AND HOW TO RESPOND TO PEOPLE WHO DON'T LIKE THEM."
BANG SI-HYUK

SM ENTERTAINMENT

Korea's largest entertainment company, SM Entertainment was established in 1995 by Lee Soo-man and is widely regarded as leading the way with K-Pop idol groups, as well as responsible for spreading Hallyu outward from the shores of South Korea. Their roster of K-Pop artists is impressive! It includes. S.E.S., BoA, TVXQ!, Super Junior, Girls' Generation, SHINee f(x), EXO, Red Velvet, NCT, and H.O.T.

> "THROUGH AUDITIONS, WE DISCOVER HIDDEN TALENT AND PUT THEM THROUGH THREE TO SEVEN YEARS OF MUSIC, DANCE, AND ACTING TRAINING IN ORDER TO CREATE A STAR THAT'S CLOSE TO PERFECTION. IT'S THROUGH THIS UNIQUE SYSTEM THAT THE HALLYU WAVE WAS CREATED." LEE SOO-MAN

JYP ENTERTAINMENT

Second only to SM, JYP Entertainment is one of the largest entertainment companies in South Korea. Founded by J. Y. Park (below, left) in 1997, JYP has transformed the lives of many trainees including Got7, Twice, Stray Kids, Itzy, Rain, G.O.D., and Wonder Girls.

RED VELVET

As delicious as the cake with the same name, Red Velvet are currently rising up the ranks of K-Pop stardom both at home and abroad.

The genuine chemistry of sisters from another mister—Irene, Seulgi, Wendy, Joy, and Yeri—made their debut for SM Entertainment in 2014, killing it at their showcase (as a quartet) as well as at their debut KCON in California with the song "Happiness," showcasing their individual talents galore. In the years since, their high-energy live performances and killer high-concept MVs have earned them many ReVelvu's—the name of their devoted fans.

Red Velvet are also one of the first K-Pop groups to delve into "dual concept" musical releases. The "Red" half of their identity encourages bright and fun pop/disco songs (singles "Ice Cream Cake," "Dumb Dumb," and "Red Flavor," for example), while the "Velvet" half of their identity allows them to explore their more mature and edgy side—"Bad Boy," for example. But while there is a dual concept in their songs, when it comes to the message they want to tell their fans, only one thing matters: confidence. "There's confidence in all of our songs," says Wendy. "We want to tell our fans that you can be whoever you want, as long as you have confidence." Well said, Wendy!

ABOVE The girls show their souls at the Seoul International Drama Awards, Seoul, September 2018.

FAR LEFT Red Velvet onstage at KCON 2015 in Los Angeles.

LEFT The RV girls wow at the 8th Gaon Chart K-Pop Awards in Seoul, January 2019.

TOP 10 KILLER MVs

1. RED FLAVOR
2. PEEK-A-BOO
3. POWER UP
4. RUSSIAN ROULETTE
5. ICE CREAM CAKE
6. WOULD U
7. AUTOMATIC
8. ROOKIE
9. BE NATURAL
10. HAPPINESS

"THERE'S CONFIDENCE IN ALL OF OUR SONGS. WE WANT TO TELL OUR FANS THAT YOU CAN BE WHOEVER YOU WANT, AS LONG AS YOU HAVE CONFIDENCE." WENDY, RED VELVET

EXO

EXO-L—the name of EXO's fandom—are the happiest fans in K-Pop for one simple reason: they have nine members of the band to love and cherish. Yes, this nonet is packed with performers—Xiumin, Suho, Lay, Baekhyun, Chen, Chanyeol, D.O., Kai, and Sehun. Which one is your bias?

Formed by SM Entertainment in 2011, EXO's fusion of pop, EDM, hip-hop, and R&B, has allowed them to make a big splash on both sides of the pond, particularly in Asia and the U.S. Only BTS are bigger at the moment, but who knows, EXO could steal the crown from BTS in the next few years thanks to the fact that the group, unlike BTS, was once two sub-units—EXO-K and EXO-M—who were brought together to form Exo, so they have twice as much star power! (If that's even possible!) "The relationship between the members, the teamwork we have, that's very important," said Suho, leader of the group. "That is what's been keeping us so successful all this while. And our love towards the fans, that's also very important to us!"

LEFT EXO pop, lock, and drop at the Mnet CountDown in Seoul, June 2013.

TOP RIGHT EXO get the thumbs up at the 28th Golden Disk Awards in Seoul, January 2014.

RIGHT A rare shot of EXO actually standing still...but not for long!

"THE RELATIONSHIP BETWEEN THE MEMBERS, THE TEAMWORK WE HAVE, THAT'S VERY IMPORTANT." SUHO, EXO

It was their debut singles, "Growl" and "Mama," that brought EXO widespread fame and success. They performed the songs at the 2018 Winter Olympics in Seoul—the only K-Pop boy group to perform at this treasured national event. Their show was so spectacular that it is too difficult to put into words here—go check it out now!

EXO are also the only K-Pop group, so far, to be in the *Guinness Book of World Records.* They have won more Daesang awards, for both Album of the Year and Artist of the Year, at the prestigious Mnet Asian Music Awards than any other K-Pop act—a huge deal! What on earth will they acheive next?

TOP 10 KILLER MVs
1. MAMA
2. BABY DON'T CRY
3. TRANSFORMER
4. OVERDOSE
5. GROWL
6. MOONLIGHT
7. MONSTER
8. CALL ME BABY
9. UNFAIR
10. STRONGER

iKON

In four years since their debut in 2015, YG Entertainment's iKON have gone from trainee idols to global icons, all thanks to their devoted iKonics, the aptly named moniker of their fans.

They are the "new kids" of K-Pop. Like several third-generation K-Pop groups, iKon were introduced to the Korean mainstream via popular reality TV shows in South Korea that mix and match group members together. It was called *Mix and Match*. Their two albums to date—*Welcome Back* and *Return*—mix bright pop rock with hip-hop accompanied by hyper visuals. The seven members—Jinhwan, Yunhyeong, Bobby, B.I., Donghyuk, Ju-ne, Chanwoo—all follow B.I.'s lead, as the main songwriter and producer. The group returned in 2019 with *New Kids*, a repackage of previous songs, as well as a new track "I'm OK," co-written by B.I. It topped iTunes global charts, but also conveyed an important message to their fans about mental health around feelings of loneliness. The song has struck a personal chord with their young listeners and helped continue the conversation that BTS started around depression and anxiety, proving that K-Pop is much more than just good songs and suits—it's about making an emotional connection with your fans.

"SINGING, DANCING, AND THE PERFORMANCE GO REALLY WELL TOGETHER. THE UNIQUE EXCITEMENT, VIBE, AND COLOR OF KOREANS ARE VERY CLEAR. WE'RE VERY PROUD OF K-POP BECAUSE IT'S A GENRE THAT REPRESENTS THE COUNTRY WE WERE BORN IN." B.I., iKON

FAR LEFT iKON share a joke onstage during their iKoncert Showtime tour, Hong Kong, May 2016.

LEFT iKON show up in style to the 25th Seoul Music Awards in Seoul, January 2016.

BELOW The icons sing their hearts out at the Gaon Chart K-Pop Awards, January 2019.

TOP 10 KILLER MVs

1. LOVE SCENARIO
2. I'M OK
3. DUMB AND DUMBER
4. MY TYPE
5. APOLOGY
6. RUBBER BAND
7. WHAT'S WRONG
8. I MISS YOU SO BAD
9. JUST ANOTHER BOY
10. EVERYTHING

TWICE

Nayeon, Jeongyeon, Momo, Sana, Jihyo, Mina, Dahyun, Chaeyoung, and Tzuyu
are the nine members who make Twice one of the most in-demand all-girl
idol groups right now in K-Pop.

They debuted back in 2015, and the release of their first single "Cheer Up" went on to become South Korea's most downloaded song of the year—an astonishing achievement for a monster rookie group. Their fanbase call themselves, rather cleverly, ONCE, and devour everything the group does, be it killer MVs such as "Dance the Night Away" or their fusion of hip-hop and jazz, described by the group as "color pop." And, of course, their group of Once fans are twice as nice. "As the group's leader, I believe our team is overflowing with energy when we're on stage," said Jihyo. "But I think it's all possible due to us getting along and our teamwork

being so great. I think that's why our team has this atmosphere of being really energetic in a way that we can feel like we're friends with fans."

One of Twice's most famous fans is the Cuban singer Camila Cabello, who revealed in 2018 that the group's infectious track, "Candy Pop" is her favorite. "Their song is stuck in my head the entire day. Like literally," the singer laughed in an interview. Cabello now even calls her mom Candy Pop in their honor. Could this signal a Camila Cabello and Twice collaboration? Let's make it happen.

ABOVE, RIGHT Twice on stage—but can you guess the song from the moves?

LEFT The Twice girls do the locomotion at the KSTAR Korea Music Festival.

OVERLEAF It's a Twice world, we're all just living in it!

"WE CAN FEEL LIKE WE'RE FRIENDS WITH FANS." JIHYO, TWICE

TOP 10 KILLER MVs

1. SIGNAL
2. DANCE THE NIGHT AWAY
3. HEART SHAKER
4. YES OR YES
5. WHAT IS LOVE?
6. KNOCK KNOCK
7. LIKEY
8. LIKE OOH-AHH
9. TT
10. CHEER UP

K-POP

DANCE CLASS

Everyone remembers the first time they did the "Gangnam Style" horse dance, don't they? Since Psy broke down music, language, and choreography barriers with his incredible first single in 2012, K-Pop, and its all-important choreography, has gone on to influence the rest of the world's love of getting down and grooving to the music—in a more spectacular fashion than ever before.

IN SYNC

When it comes to having something for everyone to enjoy, K-Pop dancing has it all. From freestyling to hip-hopping, b-boying (break dancing) to crab dancing, hand-rubbing to finger snapping, heart clutching to fist beating, flossing to flipping, K-Pop incorporates them all into something new, something never seen before. There's even emoji-inspired dancing, too! Adored for its speed, synchronicity, and stunning, high-flying acrobatics, K-Pop dancing is as skilled as it is entertaining.

TOP SIX DANCE MOVES

While there are scores—if not hundreds!—of dance moves that define K-Pop's arsenal of choreography, these are our six favorites... and the easiest to learn!

1. BODY ROLLING

Made iconic by BTS, their dance break body roll is a favorite of many K-Pop acts for its simple sexiness. The slow gyrating roll from head to toe is as transfixing as it is cool. Who does it best in BTS? Well, it's Jimin, of course! Do you agree?

2. BOTTOM SHAKING

Before twerking became a sensation in the West, Kara's "Mister," released in 2009, took synchronized booty shaking to a whole new level for K-Pop. Ever since then, butt shaking is high on the list of many choreographers' go-to moves. Sistar's "Shake It," released in 2015, is a must watch on YouTube!

"ORIGINALLY, THE BTS MEMBERS DIDN'T ALL DANCE WELL, LIKE THEY DO NOW. I WANTED TO MAKE A GROUP WITH A HIGH QUALITY IN TERMS OF PERFORMANCE. SO, ALTHOUGH OTHER ARTISTS ALSO WORK REALLY HARD, WE'RE A TEAM THAT HAS OVERCOME WITH A TREMENDOUS AMOUNT OF PRACTICE." J-HOPE, BTS LEAD DANCER

3. ARROGANT DANCING

It was the Brown Eyed Girls in 2009 who first showed the world how to perform the "arrogant dance"—swaying your hips slowly side to side, while proudly pouting—but has since found even more fame with Psy's "Gangnam Style" in 2012 and many others ever since.

KILLER K-POP CHOREOGRAPHY

CHECK THESE TRACKS OUT!
1. GANGNAM STYLE — PSY
2. DNA — BTS
3. BBOOM BBOOM — MOMOLAND
4. BUBBLE POP — HYUNA
5. MISTER — KARA
6. RING DING DONG — SHINEE
7. ABRACADABRA — BROWN EYED GIRLS
8. SORRY SORRY — SUPER JUNIOR
9. GEE — GIRL'S GENERATION
10. COMING OF AGE CEREMONY
    — PARK JI YOON

4. HIP-HOPPING

The heart of K-Pop choreography is hip-hop and urban dance moves, inspired by the 80-90s era of break dancing that traveled from the US to Korea, and inspired a generation to become obsessed with its aggressive swagger. Pretty much every K-Pop group employs hip-hop movements including body-popping and b-boying. Most notably, HyunA's "Bubble Pop!" (2011), BTS's "Hip Hop Lover" and pretty much everything Big Bang do. Indeed, Big Bang are notorious for inventing an edgy hip-hop style, which uses little choreography but lots of attitude and swagger.

5. ACROBATICS

Whether it's lifting their bodies from the ground, skipping over one another, or performing gravity-defying acrobatic back flips, diving, flipping, and somersaulting is a necessary ingredient to K-Popping. Fusing martial arts skills with high energy (and a flexible body!), performers such Jimin from BTS and Lisa and Rosé from Blackpink are famous acrobats in their groups, often flying through the air with great precision and finesse. On the flip side to their skill, Crayon Pop's "Bar Bar Bar" (2013) is, quite simply, just jumping, as if riding an imaginary pogo stick... but is still just as much fun!

6. HIP THRUSTING

Slow, fast, up, down, round and round—hip thrusting comes in all shapes and sizes. All you have to do is put your hands around your waist, bend your knees, and push your hips out violently. And most K-Pop groups are highly skilled in hip shaking. The cream of the crop are EXID, of course, who in their video "Up & Down" (2014) show us all how it's done.

SEVENTEEN

Since their impressive debut by Pledis Entertainment in May 2015, thirteen-strong Seventeen (why aren't there 17 of them?) have become serious contenders to steal the crown to become the new kings of K-Pop.

With a string of upbeat, witty, high-energy singles spreading nothing but good vibrations and unbelievable dance skills (written and choreographed by the band) and 13 of the nicest boys you'll ever hope to meet, Seventeeen have it all. In a move that is becoming increasingly common in K-Pop, the group is divided into three sub-units, each focusing on a different speciality: the hip-hop unit, the vocal unit, and the performance unit.

Over the course of two albums and seven EPs, each unit has had a chance to shine, thanks to the group's humble approach to allowing each member the opportunity to express themselves. "We constantly try to encourage each other whenever, wherever we can," revealed leader Hoshi. "When we first debuted, there were 13 of us, so it always took time to agree upon something. We've grown to understand each other as time passed, and came to learn how to take care of each other, rely on each other, and express our feelings. Our teamwork really developed further with time. That's why we never hesitate to show affection toward one another."

So, can you name all 13 members of Seventeen? Well, there's

S.Coups, Wonwoo, Mingyu, Vernon (the four of whom make up Seventeen's Hip-Hop Unit), Woozi, Jeonghan, Joshua, DK, Seungkwan (the five of whom make up the Vocal Unit), Hoshi, Jun, The8, and Dino (who make up the Performance Unit).

TOP 10 KILLER MVs

1. HEALING
2. THINKING ABOUT U
3. SHINING DIAMOND
4. DON'T WANNA CRY
5. PINWHEEL
6. AH YEAH
7. SIMPLE
8. ROCKET
9. CHOCOLATE
10. ADORE U

"I REALIZED THAT NO MATTER WHAT KIND OF MUSIC OR PERFORMANCE WE CREATE, AS LONG AS SEVENTEEN IS DOING IT THEN WE'RE JUST EXPRESSING THINGS IN OUR OWN WAY WITH OUR OWN TWIST." HOSHI, SEVENTEEN

LEFT The boys take up the entire red carpet as they arrive at the Asia Artist Awards 2018, November 2018.

ABOVE Seventeen perform at their *TEEN, AGE* album photocall.

RIGHT The Performance Unit takes flight at the 2019 Gaon Chart K-Pop Awards.

MONSTA X

With unarguably the greatest name in K-Pop, Monsta X are the bright young stars of K-Pop's future.

If you need proof, look no further than their collaboration with US superstar DJ Steve Aoki on the track "Play It Cool." Even the band were shocked by the hookup! "We heard Steve mention he wanted to collaborate with us, and it was shocking," revealed lead rapper I.M. "It was just so dope. This legend in the industry, the worldwide famous DJ, wanted to work with us, with us? It was amazing, but I thought that was it, just a wish. But then it actually happened!" Check out the MV now—wow!

ARE YOU A MONBEBE? MONSTA X'S FANS NAME IS TAKEN FROM "MON" MEANING "MY" AND "BEBE" MEANING "BABY" IN FRENCH!

"THE RELATIONSHIP WITH OUR FANS HAS GOTTEN DEEPER AFTER ALL THESE YEARS. TIME HAS PASSED FAST AND A LOT OF THINGS HAVE CHANGED, WHICH HAS MADE OUR RELATIONSHIP STRONGER. OUR FANS ARE EVERYTHING TO US, THEY SEE US PERFORM, THEY SEE US GROW. THE REASON WE ARE PERFORMING EVERY DAY IS THEM AND ONLY THEM." I.M., MONSTA X

FAR LEFT The Monsta say hi to their monbebe's at WiLD 94.9's FM's Jingle Ball in San Francisco, December 2018.

ABOVE Kihyun, Shownu, Jooheon, Hyungwon, Minhyuk, Wonho, and I.M in New York City, December 2018..

LEFT Monsta X strut their stuff at KIIS FM's Jingle Ball 2018, California, November 30.

Debuting through the 2015 reality show *No.Mercy*, Monsta X's seven members (Shownu, Wonho, Minhyuk, Kihyun, Hyungwon, Joohoney, and I.M.) are in complete synchronization with each other as shown in their pinpoint choreography, achieved through hours of practicing together. But, as Monsta X have learned, when it comes to breathtaking choreography, sometimes less is more. "When you see difficult choreography, you want to try learning it, and you think of it as a challenge," revealed Minhyuk. "Like when we were trainees. Difficult choreography looks hard but cool. At the same time, it does seem like it's important for choreography to be easy to learn, so fans can dance along." With MVs such as "Jealousy" notorious for it's high-octane choreography, even Monsta X admit that some of their dance moves are "too hard" and even the camera can't keep up. So, do you know all the moves? Because if you do... you could be an idol!

TOP 10 KILLER MVs
1. HIEUT
2. SHINE FOREVER
3. RUSH
4. BEAUTIFUL
5. INTERSTELLAR
6. STUCK
7. TRESPASS
8. ALL IN
9. FIGHTER
10. JEALOUSY

ASTRO

Despite missing the opportunity to call themselves Astronauts—and opting to call themselves Arohas instead!—Astro fans have every right to be a happy bunch: their favorite band is getting bigger and bigger with each new comeback.

This very good-looking monster rookie group first debuted in 2016, as part of Fantagio's roster, with the track "Hide & Seek." Since then, the six-piece (JinJin, MJ, Cha Eun-woo, Moon Bin, Rocky, and Yoon San-ha) have wowed their growing legion of fans both at home and abroad, quickly being regarded as one of the best new K-Pop groups of their debut year. While their MVs and vocals are on-point, naturally, making them sound and feel good, Astro also enjoy looking good, too. Makeup, hair, and fashion are equally important to the band as their music, but not because they are vain—because looking good means feeling confident. And when you feel confident, the world is yours! "Whether you bring a song or album in front of the audience, I think hair and makeup is the best way to express ourselves," leader JinJin says. Bandmate, Cha Eun Woo, agrees: "Since I'm a celebrity, I want to be very pretty on screen!" he says. He's nailing it.

ABOVE Astro stoke a pose before the Taipei Star Light Concert, March 2019.

LEFT Look at the stars, look how they sign for you. Astro attend a press conference in Hong Kong, November 2017.

TOP 10 KILLER MVs
1. ALL NIGHT
2. HIDE AND SEEK
3. BABY
4. ALWAYS YOU
5. CONFESSION
6. LOVE WHEEL
7. BLOOM
8. BUTTERFLY
9. CALL OUT
10. CRAZY SEXY COOL

"I WANT US TO BE TOGETHER FOR TEN, TWENTY YEARS, FOR A LONG TIME—JUST LIKE NOW." JINJIN, ASTRO

GOT7

Seven may be their lucky number, but Got7 have never needed luck. They have obtained all their global success by being the most hard working boy band in K-Pop. Today, their blood, sweat, and tears has paid off—they've got it all.

2018 was a very good year for Got7. After working hard since their debut drop in 2014, the septet received the opportunity to travel to the United States on their *Eyes on You* world tour, culminating in a show at the prestigious Barclays Center in Brooklyn, New York. No other K-Pop group had ever played there. This was a big deal, and proof that the boys had made it—finally—after four and a half years of being together as trainees, struggling to find the moment to debut. But all that time together as trainees is now paying off big time: the boys' genuine chemistry had endeared them to a massive fanbase, called iGot7s (because 7 is a lucky number in Korea). "The Barclays Center is just so big. It's truly a dream," remembers Youngjae of the biggest moment of their career so far. "A year ago I was there to see Kendrick Lamar, and I can't believe we're on the other side of the stage now. At the end, it's all thanks to the fans." The group's meteoric rise to the top of the K-Pop ladder has given the boys an opportunity to appreciate just how far they have come, how lucky they are, and how proud they are to represent their country doing something they love. "In some places, we're the first K-Pop group that can perform at these arenas and sell

TOP 10 KILLER MVs

1. FLY
2. NEVER EVER
3. CONFESSION SONG
4. YOU ARE
5. GIRLS, GIRLS, GIRLS
6. STOP, STOP IT
7. HARD CARRY
8. IF YOU DO
9. JUST RIGHT
10. A

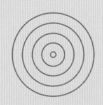

> "WHEN WE WORK FOR GOT7 WE'RE SEVEN INDIVIDUALS, WHO WORK IN UNISON. WE'RE A RAINBOW THAT OFFERS SEVEN DIFFERENT COLORS."
> JACKSON, GOT7

them out," reveals BamBam. "It's an honor and, as a K-Pop artist, I feel like another group can get some energy from us, too. K-Pop is not just Got7; we're all family. Got7, another group, different companies—we'll start right now, and later we'll make K-Pop bigger so another group can perform here, too."

Got7 leader JB, along with Mark, Jackson, Jinyoung, Youngjae, BamBam, and Yugyeom, received praise early following their debut, thanks crucially to their kicking butt on the dance floor during their dynamic and high-energy stage performances and choreography that includes a lot of acrobatic martial arts tricking and ridiculous dance breaks.

RIGHT The boys of Got7 display their international credentials by attending a Build Series event in New York City to discuss their upcoming tour.

LEFT Got7 show they got serious style in Shanghai, January 2018.

THE SEVEN STYLES OF K-POP

K-Pop idol groups are famous for their often extravagant, garish, and stylish (take your pick!) choice of outfits, often adhering to the acts' own carefully selected and designed color palette. For your viewing pleasure, we have identified the seven styles of K-Pop that every idol group treats us to every time they step out into the world...

1. SUIT AND TIE

Every now and again, for prestigious events, your favorite K-Pop band likes to look well-tailored and stylish in a suit and tie.

2. ABSOLUTELY BONKERS

Every idol has a completely crazy costume in their wardrobe... and usually more than just one!

3. IDENTICAL

When every member in an idol group wants to look identical to their bandmate... this happens!

4. RELAXED

Some days its just nice to chill in something comfortable...

5. EDGY

For those moments when you need to look cool and alternative...

6. CUTE

Some days looking *aeygo* is all that matters...

7. FUNNY

It will be tough to find an idol group without a good sense of humor when it comes to their fashion choices...

MAMAMOO

Many girl idol groups have ascended to the status of global icons in the past several years—we're looking at you Blackpink, Twice, and GFriend!—but none are as carefree and feel good as Mamamoo!

With their super upbeat songs and technicolor MVs, a fusion of R&B, jazz, and retro genres, stylish costume choices, and laidback personalities, Solar, Hwasa, Wheein, and Moonbyul are four sisters, and solo artists, who are putting the fun back into funky K-Pop.

Following their debut in 2014 with the single "Mr. Ambiguous" (what a tune!), Mamamoo have gained much recognition for the strength of their live and studio vocal performances—these girls are talented, for sure. The secret to their success, though, is not in their voices or their choice of stage outfits—it's in their chemistry, forged through a difficult time trying to make their debut perfect. "Our secret key is to confront each other when needed," revealed Hwasa. "We confronted each other often, and after going through those times, we can now communicate with each other by just looking at each other's eyes."

Since 2015, the four girls have become role models throughout the world and are often cited as influences by the newest generation of K-Pop groups debuting in 2019. Hwasa's advice to all trainees and MooMoos (the sweet name for their fans!) wanting to be idols is simple: persevere! "We went through countless auditions, too, but it's important to enjoy it, and it's also important to work hard," she revealed. "And not give up. I think that continuously working hard can lead to a lot of opportunities. So I really want to cheer on everyone who is preparing to become a singer. Don't give up!'

LEFT Mamamoo perform a stunning showcase for their mini album *Red Moon*, July 2018.

ABOVE Put your arms in the air like you just don't care! Mamamoo on stage in Taipei, September 2018.

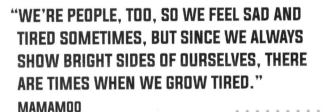

"WE'RE PEOPLE, TOO, SO WE FEEL SAD AND TIRED SOMETIMES, BUT SINCE WE ALWAYS SHOW BRIGHT SIDES OF OURSELVES, THERE ARE TIMES WHEN WE GROW TIRED."
MAMAMOO

TOP 10 KILLER MVs
1. MR. AMBIGUOUS
2. TALLER THAN YOU
3. UM OH AH YEAH
4. YOU'RE THE BEST
5. GIRL CRUSH
6. PIANO MAN
7. EMOTION
8. WOO HOO
9. PEPPERMINT CHOCOLATE
10. DÉCALCOMANIE

EXID

EXID, an abbreviation of Exceed in Dreaming, are incredibly dreamy, which is precisely what you need in a "girl crush" K-Pop act—a group designed to look good and make their fans, known as *Legos*, feel good.

They rose to prominence in 2012, when their first single "Up & Down" went viral (check out the famous fan-recording of a live performance of the song and you'll know why!). EXID members Solji, LE, Hani, Hyelin, and Jeonghwa are vocalists, visualists, rappers, and dancers who had to fight hard to debut, following incidents and accidents that delayed their delivery to the world for more than two long years. "We spent our hardships together," LE revealed recently. "And before we were actually famous, we were able to go through all the times together. That's why our friendship became something stronger."

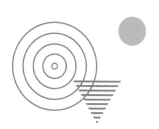

LEFT EXID arrive in New Jersey for KCON! in June 2018.

ABOVE The group attend the "Hello Future-GMIC X Annual Event" in Beijing, April 2016

"BEAUTY ISN'T ABOUT HAVING A PRETTY FACE. IT'S ABOUT HAVING A PRETTY MIND, A PRETTY HEART, AND A PRETTY SOUL." EXID

TOP 10 KILLER MVs

1. L.I.E
2. GOOD GOOD BYE
3. HOT PINK
4. I FEEL GOOD
5. EVERY NIGHT
6. WHOZ THAT GIRL
7. NIGHT RATHER THAN DAY
8. CREAM
9. AH YEAH
10. UP AND DOWN

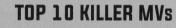

TVXQ!

Of the very few popular duos in K-Pop, TVXQ! are a rare entity indeed, considering the staggering success they have achieved together.

TVXQ! STANDS FOR TONG VFANG XIEN QI, OR "RISING GODS OF THE EAST"!

Bandmates U-Know Yunho and Max Changmin were conjured together by SM Entertainment in 2003, when they were originally part of a five-piece boy band. Since then, the pair have won almost every award in K-Pop, including Golden Disk Award for Album of the Year in 2006. For the first decade of their career, TVQX! remained at the top of pops as one of Asia's most cherished acts, often regarded as "K-Pop royalty" or the "godfathers of K-Pop."

After a decade of being out of the K-Pop spotlight, U-Know Yunho and Max Changmin returned as TVXQ!, following military service (compulsory in Korea) and solo careers.

"At one point, the thought occurred to me that it is a possibility that the younger generation won't know us," Yunho admitted when news broke of TVXQ!'s comeback. But those fears disappeared as soon as news of their comeback broke the internet. In the time the duo have been away, the K-Pop landscape has completely transformed to be a worldwide phenomenon. But, that's only because first-generation groups like TVXQ! helped pioneer K-Pop and opened the door for future artists. "It's an honor and personally satisfying to know that some artists have built their dream of becoming K-Pop stars by watching us," Changmin said. K-Pop started with TVXQ!... and now the duo returns to a heroes' welcome! It's good to have them back.

TOP LEFT TVXQ!, in their original five-man line-up, celebrate the release of "Mirotic," September 2008.

BOTTOM LEFT Two's company: the new-look TVXQ! perform together in 2018.

RIGHT The duo look impossibly suave in their complementary tuxes.

TOP 10 KILLER MVs

1. WRONG NUMBER
2. FIGHTING SPRIT OF THE EAST
3. ANDROID
4. SPELLBOUND
5. KEEP YOUR HEAD DOWN
6. PURPLE LINE
7. BALLOONS
8. MIROTIC
9. CATCH ME
10. RISING SUN

"I WANT TVXQ! TO KEEP PUSHING OUR SONIC BOUNDARIES, EXPERIMENTING WITH NEW GENRES/CONCEPTS, AND KEEP GROWING AS AN ARTIST, SO THAT WAY WE CAN BE A GROUP THAT IS LOVED BY ALL TYPES OF MUSIC FANS AND ULTIMATELY BECOME ONE OF THE LONGEST-RUNNING LIVE PERFORMERS." U-KNOW YUNHO, TVXQ!

GFRIEND

Gfriend has been their Buddy's best friend since they arrived on the scene in 2015. Today, they have transformed from one of Korea's most promising rookie groups to full-on champions of K-Pop. *Mansae!*

They're beloved by their Buddy's for simply being in sync with each other in every way, as well as the sweetness of their synth pop songs such as "Glass Bead," "Fingertip," and "Rain in the Summertime." Bandmates Sowon, Yerin, Eunha, Yuju, SinB, and Umji are genuine BFFs in real life, adding to their cheerful happy-go-lucky vibe—a result of finding worldwide mega-success, despite debuting from a smaller management company, and not one of the big boys such as YG, JYP, or SM. This makes them extra lucky!

The group released their first album *LOL* in July 2016, but it is with their follow-up *The Awakening* that the rest of the world got woke to the girls' fun charms, the secret to their success, or so Sowon says: "I would say that something that made us stand out from other groups is that we try to incorporate a variety of charms into our music. For example, choreography-wise we have a very energetic vibe going on, but musically it's more innocent, happy. A girlish sort of style. If you look at our wardrobe choices, too, it's something else. All these different facets of everything that constitutes our group, you can see that it shows very eclectic elements of our group, and I think that's what makes us interesting and fun."

ABOVE GFriend strike their best James Bond poses to celebrate the release of "Parallel," August 2017.

LEFT GFriend get in line at KCON, Los Angeles, July 2016.

TOP 10 KILLER MVs

1. WAVE
2. SUMMER RAIN
3. LOVE WHISPER
4. SUNNY SUMMER
5. TIME FOR THE MOON NIGHT
6. GLASS BEAD
7. ME GUSTAS TU
8. FINGERTIP
9. ROUGH
10. NAVILLERA

NEXT GEN K-POP

The next generation of K-Pop is always ready to show the groups of today what tomorrow looks like! Every year scores of new groups emerge as the new faces of K-Pop, but only a handful break through and achieve global recognition. Here's a shoutout to the rookie groups on the edge of success.

CHERRY BULLET

Ten-piece girl group Cherry Bullet (below) debuted in January 2019 with their single album *Let's Play Cherry Bullet*. Members Hae Yoon, Yu Ju, Mi Rae, Bo Ra, Ji Won, Kokoro, Re Mi, Chae Rin, Lin Lin, and May are over the moon that after time spent as trainees at FNC agency, they now have a shot at K-Pop fame. "At first it didn't feel real, but as we get to perform more on stage and meet our fans it will become more realistic," said the group in unison at their debut showcase. "We're so happy that we debuted as Cherry Bullet and our days have been filled with delight ever since. We want to be an artist who can give positive energy to the audience with various charms we have prepared for them!" But what on earth is a Cherry Bullet, I hear you ask? Good Question! "Cherry Bullet means that we will pierce through one's heart with our 'cherry'-like loveliness and charm. Along with our talents, filled with energy that is as strong as a bullet!"

TOP 3 KILLER MVs
1. Q&A
2. VIOLET
3. STICK OUT

"I DON'T WANT TO BE LIKE OTHER IDOL GROUPS IN KOREA. I WANT TO DO SOMETHING NEW. I DON'T REALLY GET INSPIRED BY OTHER MUSIC, I JUST SOLELY THINK ABOUT EACH OF THE MEMBERS AND GAIN INSPIRATION FROM THAT." SOYEON, (G)I-DLE

TOP 10 KILLER MVs
1. SENORITA
2. LATATA
3. RELAY
4. BLOW YOUR MIND
5. DON'T TEXT ME
6. PUT IT STRAIGHT
7. UPGRADE
8. MAZE
9. WHAT'S YOUR NAME
10. MERMAID

(G)I-DLE

Three months after their debut in Summer 2018, (G)I-DLE (above) have already secured success in the United States. That's a monster rookie move! Girl-Idle or (G)I-DLE as they call themselves are the hottest ticket in K-Poptown and have their sights set on BTS-esque success. "We really respect BTS as artists," revealed Soyeon, on behalf of Minni, Soonjin, Yuqi, Miyeon, and Shuhua. "Since BTS did help and introduce so many people to so many artists, we're influenced by them, too. We would like to also strive for a similar path." This band has big goals!

In Soyeon, the group's producer and principal songwriter, (G)I-DLE have a leader who has placed huge expectation on her songs and her group's abilities—wanting to smash the mold of what it means to be a Korean idol group, and what they can mean to their fans. She has the support of her bandmates. "Since we have a lot of charms to still show, I want the fans' expectations to be higher than ever. The key word I want fans to have when thinking about us is 'reliable,' and that you can depend on us," says Soonjin.

TOP 5 KILLER MVs
1. CROWN
2. CAT & DOG
3. OUR SUMMER
4. NAP OF A STAR
5. BLUE ORANGEADE

TXT

TXT, or Tomorrow X Together if you prefer the long version, is the second boy band in six years to debut by Big Hit Entertainment. The other band was BTS. No pressure, boys! The quintet of seventeen year olds, Yeonjun, Soobin, Beomgyu, Taehyun, and Huening Kai are being regarded as BTS little brothers-in-arms (but with a different concept to their bigger brothers) following their debut in March 2019 with the EP *The Dream Chapter: Star*, which went into the top album charts in scores of countries. "We were really surprised at the amount of love given to us and while it feels undeserved, it makes us want to work even harder," the boys said upon their debut. What do you think, will TXT be the next big thing?

ITZY

Fresh from their debut showcase in February 2019, ITZY are finally ready to show the world just how much K is in their pop! Created by JYP Entertainment, the group have been positioned as an edgier alternative to idol girl groups. Their debut MV "It'z Different" certainly showed off some elements new to the genre. The quintet—Yeji, Lia, Ryujin, Chaeryeong, and Yuna—are hoping to hit the big time in 2019, thanks to the impressive, and sparkly, introductions they made during their debut showcase. They even have their own motto: "All In Us, we are ITZY." What does it mean? Well, Yeji will tell us: "It means that we have everything you are looking for in us. We would like to display an aura that you couldn't quite see from other groups before." We can't wait to see what Itzy has in store for us...

KILLER MVs
1. DALLA DALLA
2. WANT IT?

MOMOLAND

From reality TV stardom to K-Pop chart domination, Momoland have come a long way in just a few short years. Rocking a quirky but hugely danceable sound, with the styles to match, don't be surprised to see them blow up worldwide soon.

In 2018, Momoland had the breakout success of a smash-hit single that took the K-Pop world by surprise. You know what song I'm talking about—"BBoom BBoom!" With its boppy hooks, infectious positivity, and bouncy MV choreography that even spawned a new dance craze, the song catapulted the nonet (Hyebin, Yeonwoo, Jane, Taeha, Nayun, Daisy, JooE, Ahin, and Nancy) to become the K-Pop group everyone was talking about. Their follow-ups—"BAAM" and "I'm So Hot"—have repeated the same formula, giving Momoland a quirky, colorful space of their own to work in. Discovered in 2016 through the TV show *Finding Momoland*, the girls have survived some tough times in order to achieve success. "Because 'BBoom

BBoom' has received so much love, we couldn't help but worry whether 'BAAM' would sit well with the listeners this time round. But we feel that this is a fun song that displays our distinct and funky style, so we hope that people will enjoy it as much as 'BBoom BBoom!'" What Momoland do next is anyone's guess, but let's hope they don't remain one hit wonders...

ABOVE Momoland strike a pose on stage in Seoul, June 2018.

LEFT The girls "Freeze" onstage in Seoul, August 2017.

TOP 10 KILLER MVs

1. BAAM
2. BBOOM BBOOM
3. I'M SO HOT
4. WONDERFUL LOVE
5. ONLY ONE YOU
6. FREEZE
7. CURIOUS
8. FLY
9. SAME SAME
10. LIGHT UP

"THERE AREN'T REALLY ANY CONFLICTS BETWEEN US. I THINK WASHING IS PROBABLY THE BIGGEST CONCERN FOR US BECAUSE THERE ARE ONLY TWO BATHROOMS IN OUR DORM, SO WE HAVE TO FIGURE OUT WHO TO GO FIRST EVERY MORNING!" DAISY, MOMOLAND

IU

K-Pop's leading lady IU (born Lee Ji-eun) has transformed from bubblegum pop princess to serious solo singer-songwriter, respected and beloved in equal measure, ever since her debut at the age of fifteen in 2007.

Her sophomore single "Good Day," the lead release from her aptly titled 2010 album *Real*, propelled her from rookie trainee to serious superstar almost overnight... becoming the bestselling track on South Korea's Gaon Digital Chart—until Psy's "Gangnam Style" came along, that is. Touted abroad as Korea's "Little Sister," IU is the girl-next-door superstar that everyone adores, a vital ingredient as to why, more than ten years and four albums later, IU has remained at the top of K-Pop and been allowed to mature as a musician. Today, IU now sings serious stories of love and life, instead of sweet little nothings. Due to her longevity in the industry, IU was voted the most popular idol and artist among South Koreans in 2017—a fact matched by one simple truth: IU has topped the Korean chart more than any other artist since 2010, outperforming BTS, Girls' Generation, and Big Bang, three of the bestselling K-Pop groups of all time! All hail the queen of K-Pop!

RIGHT The queen of K-Pop poses, September 2008.

TOP 10 KILLER MVs
1. MARSHMALLOW
2. PALETTE
3. TWENTY-THREE
4. THE RED SHOES
5. BEAUTIFUL DANCER
6. YOU KNOW
7. BOO
8. SEA OF MOONLIGHT
9. YOU & I
10. GOOD DAY

NCT

Striking while the iron is hot in the United States, NCT are more than just the sum of their twenty-seven individual parts. Yes, that's right—there are twenty-seven members in NCT.

In fact, there are so many members, we don't have room to mention all of their names! However, the high concept behind NCT is that the group is unit based and rotational, meaning that the band offers a little something for everyone with each new unit, sub-unit, and song or EP release. It doesn't matter whether you're a fan of positive pop, grinding hip-hop, experimental EDM, or tear-duct busting balladry—NCT have got you covered. Their name, NCT, was coined by SM Entertainment founder Lee Soo-man to denote Neo Culture Technology, a concept that describes the group's ability to have an endless amount of members, divided into multiple sub-units and based all around the world.

"Because there are so many members, I always feel supported," member Doyoung said in 2018. "It's always fun and energetic, and we're always ready to take on just about anything. We're all so close that even when we go eat or have some free time to play, we usually spend it together. The only bad thing I can think of is that we take so long to pick a menu when we go out to eat together!"

TOP RIGHT Taeil, Johnny, Taeyong, Yuta, Doyoung, Jaehyun, Winwin, Jungwoo, Mark, Haechan look handsome on the American Music Awards red carpet, Los Angeles, October 2018.

RIGHT NCT make shapes at MBC Korean Music Wave concert, Seoul, September 2018.

OVERLEAF NCT perform on *Jimmy Kimmel Live*, Los Angeles, October 2018. But can you guess the song?

TOP 10 KILLER MVs
1. THE 7TH SENSE
2. FIRE TRUCK
3. WE YOUNG
4. SWITCH
5. BOSS
6. LIMITLESS
7. CHEWING GUM
8. BABY DON'T STOP
9. MY FIRST & LAST
10. WITHOUT YOU

"WE'RE ALL SO CLOSE THAT EVEN WHEN WE GO EAT OR HAVE SOME FREE TIME TO PLAY, WE USUALLY SPEND IT TOGETHER."
DOYOUNG, NCT